BSA
BANTAM

ALL MODELS

Roy Bacon

First published in the United Kingdom by:
Niton Publishing
PO Box 3. Ventnor. Isle of Wight PO38 2AS

Acknowledgements
The author would like to thank those who
helped this book by supplying the photo-
graphs. Most came from the EMAP archives
or *Motor Cycle News* by courtesy of the
editor. Malcolm Gough and some
from the Mick Woollett archive.
My thanks to all.

This edition published 1995 by
The Promotional Reprint Company Ltd.
exclusively for Selecta Book Limited.
Roundway, Devizes. Wiltshire SN10 2HR
and Reed Editions in Australia.

ISBN 1 85648 311 8

Printed in Hong Kong

Bantams on tour down under in Australia, just one of the many countries where the model found friends.

Contents

Introduction

The BSA Bantam was built from 1948 to 1971 in 123, 148 and 172 cc capacities, with a variety of cycle parts, and for road, competition and trail use. It was possibly the most successful British machine of all time in terms of numbers built and served its owners, many of them learners and commuters, well, despite some weaknesses.

Yet the Bantam was not a BSA design at all but was based on the pre-war DKW RT125, which had been taken over as part of the war reparations. That DKW layout was also used by the American Harley-Davidson, Russian Voskhod and Japanese Yamaha, so was highly regarded worldwide, while DKW themselves kept on with it in their post-war range, but in a new plant in West Germany. Their old factory at Zschopau lay in the East and was renamed IFA, and then MZ, but it continued to build models based on the old RT125 for many a year.

Truly a universal motorcycle.

Bob Currie out road testing a 1962 Bantam D1 which was little altered from the first model but was soon to go from the range.

The First Bantam

The Bantam was launched in March 1948 as an engine and gearbox unit to meet an export order, and it was not until June of that year that a complete machine appeared. That, too, was for export only at first, but it was introduced on to its home market later in the year.

The engine was a built in unit with its three-speed gearbox and was a mirror-image of the DKW down to the profile of the head and barrel. The few differences made were to accommodate the larger British flywheel magneto, allow the fitting of an Amal carburettor and convert the dimensions to inches to suit the BSA machine tools. The mirror reversal of the engine placed the gear pedal and kickstarter on the right, as was usual for British machines.

The original Bantam engine had a 58 mm stroke, which was retained by the later, larger versions, so was common to all, and the first engine combined this with a 52 mm bore to give a 123 cc capacity. The unit was based on a cast aluminium crankcase, split vertically on the cylinder centre line, with a locating spigot formed round the flywheel chamber. A dozen or so screws held the two halves together, and alignment was assisted by hollow

First year Bantam with flat silencer, exhaust pipe under footrest and shovel mudguard; simple, sturdy and effective.

The DKW RT125 whose engine was adopted in mirror image by the Bantam as part of war reparations.

dowels fitted in the upper front and rear engine mounting holes. These holes, together with the two lower ones, were also to remain common to all models and years, which makes it very easy to change Bantam engines around.

The crankshaft was built up with rather large diameter flywheels.

These made the engine a little taller than it might have been but in many respects the construction was well in advance of its British contemporaries. Each flywheel was a full circle with the balance weight forged into a hollow in the outer face, but was smooth on its inner face and periphery. The hollow was closed off

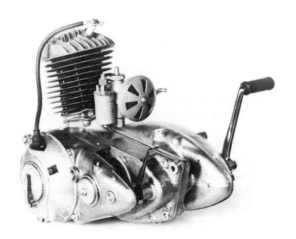

First version of the 123 cc Bantam engine had this Wipac generator which was soon altered. The arm behind the gearbox sprocket is a gear indicator.

7

The pre-war DKW factory finished up in the Russian zone after the war so this RT125 copy did not come as much of a suprise.

with a thin steel disc, which fitted into a machined recess and was retained by centre punching.

The mainshafts and shouldered crankpin were pressed into the flywheels and the complete crankshaft ran in three ball-race main bearings. One went on the left, with an oil seal outboard of it, and the others on the right with a seal between them. The big end bearing was a single row of uncaged rollers that ran directly on the pin and in the hardened eye of the connecting rod. This was a steel stamping with a phosphor bronze small end bush.

The slightly domed, aluminium-alloy piston was fitted to the rod

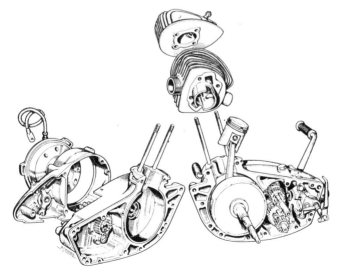

Bantam D1 engine unit exploded to show the major parts which were to serve so many riders so well.

with a fully-floating, hollow gudgeon pin retained by wire circlips. There were two plain, pegged rings so the design was modern and lacked the deflector on the crown, common in two-stroke engines of the pre-war period. Cut-aways on each side, below the gudgeon pin bosses, matched corresponding openings in the cylinder.

The cast iron cylinder was inclined forward a little and spigoted into the crankcase. Together with the light alloy cylinder head, it was

the carburettor and incorporated a strangler choke for cold starting. The exhaust port was at the front, but its outlet was offset to the right to clear the frame downtube, so the port tract was formed to suit. The outlet was threaded externally for an exhaust pipe nut. A transfer port was cast into each side of the cylinder with its exit window angled to direct the mixture. Each was fed via a transfer passage cast into the crankcase, and the gas flow was assisted by the cut-aways in each

Harley-Davidson also made a copy of the DKW which they called the Hummer and built in two sizes; this is an early 125

fitted on to four long studs screwed into the crankcase, with nuts to retain them. At first, metal-to-metal joints were used, but within weeks a base gasket appeared, although the head joint remained as it was for some years.

The cylinder had an inlet stub at the rear, and this was angled to carry a clip-fitting, single lever, 5/8 in. bore Amal carburettor in an upright position. An air cleaner was fitted to

side of the cylinder spigot and piston.

The cylinder head had a part-spherical combustion chamber, which gave the engine a 6.5:1 compression ratio, and its sparking plug lay back at an angle on the centre line. There was no spigot between the head and barrel, but the cooling fins of both had a common line.

The engine was petroil lubricated, and the oil mist was led to the left and inner right main bearings by holes drilled down from the transfer passages; while the outer right main was looked after by transmission oil. The connecting rod had slots cut in the big-end eye so that the oil mist could reach the rollers, and the same mist kept the piston and small-end healthy.

Ignition was by a Wipac flywheel magneto and generator mounted on the left-hand end of the crankshaft. This had the rotor inboard of the stator, which was supported by a casting that extended back to carry the clutch mechanism.The casting

was positioned by two dowels, and the stator was clamped to it with a degree of rotational adjustment to allow the ignition timing to be varied.

The rotor was keyed to a tapered section of the mainshaft with the points cam mounted on the extreme end of the shaft, where it was held by a small screw. This made the shaft rather fragile, thanks to the combination of the tapped hole, small parallel diameter and a keyway, so care is needed when using a puller to remove the rotor.

The stator carried both ignition

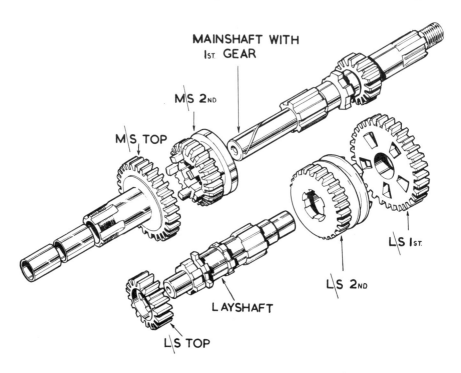

Three speed Bantam gearbox details; reversal of the layshaft gear means that only two speeds can be selected.

The simple and basic D1 in its 1953 form with fresh front mudguard but otherwise little altered from its launch.

and lighting coils, plus the contact points, and was bushed to support the mainshaft. The bush really had little chance of controlling the long, whippy shaft carrying the heavy rotor, but it was better than nothing. In practice, the stator did not fit the casting all that well, so it would take up a position dictated by the bush rather than anything else.

A small cover, held in place by a spring clip, concealed the points and an adaptor, fitted in the top of the stator, connected the high tension lead to the internal coil. A further connection was used for the direct lighting which, thus, only

Competition D1 at a Classic Bike show in the late 1980's with cylinder head with decompressor, raised saddle and tilted silencer.

Bantam on show at the Schoolboys' Own Exhibition in early 1953 where it was rigged to test reaction times.

worked while the engine was running.

The primary drive went on the right with a sprocket keyed to the crankshaft and driving the clutch through a single strand chain. The clutch was very good and had three friction plates with cork inserts, two plain plates and a pressure plate. They were clamped by six non-adjustable compression springs and the assembly was held together by one large circlip. This fitted into the clutch drum which ran on a bronze flanged bush and against a thrust washer of the same material.

The clutch spring plate was soon amended so that a light flanged disc could be fixed to it. The flange fitted closely over the drum to prevent this spreading under centrifugal loads, for this might have released the circlip that held the clutch together. All Bantams had this feature from then on.

The clutch was mounted on the right-hand end of the gearbox mainshaft and lifted by a quick thread mechanism with central adjustment screw on the left. This moved a pushrod and mushroom within the shaft, and the operating cable swept in under the magneto housing to a cast-in socket. The inner cable was connected to an arm riveted to the quick-thread screw, which was a loose fit in its mating housing, but worked very well despite this.

Being of the cross-over type, the gearbox sprocket and sleeve gear went on the left, but otherwise it was conventional. The layshaft was placed below the mainshaft and ran in bushes, but there were ball races for the clutch end of the mainshaft and the sleeve gear. This had an oil seal outboard of it in a pressed steel housing and bushes in its bore.

The change mechanism was to the rear of the gears and selected the ratios by moving the two middle gears as a pair. A simple plate did this and also indexed them with a spring and ball working in notches. The positive stop mechanism moved this plate and had the usual centring spring on its pedal shaft, which emerged on the right to give an up-for-up change. On the left, the

mechanism included a shaft with a small pointer attached, to indicate the engaged gear.

It was a good gearbox, which worked well once the index notch for second gear was deepened. The snags were caused by the pedal spring and gear ratios,the former being inside the crankcase, which had to be split to replace the spring if it failed. The ratio problem was due to too large a jump from second to top, which could make hill climbing tedious.

The combination of the ratio gap and the pedal movement could, and did catch riders out, especially those used to the more popular down-for-up change of those times. They would run to peak revs in second, forget, and change into bottom instead of top. Even if they then remembered, and held the clutch in,

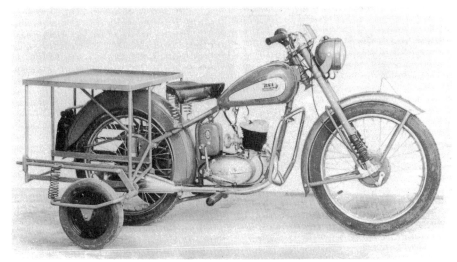

Owners often adapted the Bantam in some way to suit their needs and this is just one example worked on a 1953 D1.

Plunger frame D3 from 1954 with the heavier front forks, battery lighting and electric horn.

the effect was dramatic; if the clutch went home it was common to strip all the teeth from the mainshaft first gear, which meant a new shaft.

The kickstart mechanism worked on the back of the clutch drum and, thus, gave primary starting, which was most useful to novice and expert alike. We all stall the engine at some time, and the ability to kick-start without searching for neutral can be a face-saver in traffic. The mechanism comprised a gear wheel with spring ratchet on the back of the drum and a quadrant to mesh with it. This was fitted to a hollow shaft, which ran in the chaincase outer casting and carried the kickstart lever. Through it ran the gearchange pedal shaft, and it was

Magneto and final drive side of a 1954 D3 with the more extensive engine fins and here with battery and electric horn.

Another learner ties L plates on an early Bantam which would stand up well to this treatment. The 'bobby-dodger' cycle front lamp was a common sight even for this 1955 picture.

returned by a clock spring, which was accessible once the cover had been removed.

Both gearbox and primary drive shared the same oil, so there was a passage in the right-hand crankcase casting between the two chambers. The same oil also served the outer right-side main bearing and had to be poured in via a small, angled filler in the top of the crankcase. This was always an awkward task, but the filler plug had a dipstick attached, to let you know your progress. There was a common drain plug for both chambers, and a smaller one for the engine crankcase.

When the complete machine appeared, this engine unit went into a simple welded loop frame. There were mounting plates at front and rear to pick up on the four fixings, the top front one providing positive location, while the rear ones were slotted to allow for manufacturing variations. Small lugs were welded on for the seat, tank, rear mudguard, toolbox and chainguard, with a larger one for the footrest bar. This rod, with distance tubes and footrest rubbers, also carried the centre stand and rear brake pedal, both of which pivoted on the tubes. The stand was retained by a spring clip bolted to the seat tube end, and the pedal had a return spring fitted to it.

The frame was rigid and had simple telescopic front forks with internal springs, grease lubrication and no damping. The top yoke was a pressing to which the speedometer and the split handlebar

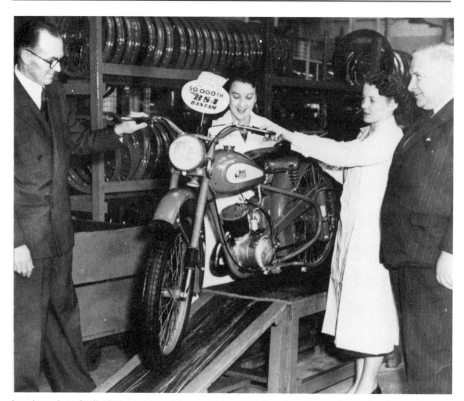

It only took to April 1951 to get to this machine which has the plunger frame but keeps the remote lever for the lights control and the bulb horn.

clamps were fixed, the bars themselves having the brake and clutch lever pivots welded on. The bottom yoke carried a bracket on its clamp bolts for the headlamp, and its steering stem formed part of the horn, the bulb being screwed into the top end and the outlet cone attached to the bottom.

The wheels had offset hubs with 5in. single-leading-shoe drum brakes, which proved highly effective. The rear hub had the sprocket riveted to it, and its brake rod operated directly from the pedal. The hubs were spoked to 19 in. steel rims carrying 2.75 in. section tyres. The front one was protected by a mudguard with a very deep valance, which carried the number plate on each side. This guard was fixed to the upper fork legs, with a simple cross-stay on each side, and, thus, was sprung. At the rear, the mudguard had a valance that varied in depth, reducing to nothing at the tail, its main support being the rear carrier.

The saddle went in front of this, but BSA never offered a pillion pad, although there were optional pillion footrests in due course. The accessory trade soon filled this gap with a pad that clipped to the carrier. A small toolbox went under the saddle, to the rear of the air cleaner, and could carry a selection of spanners and a spare plug or two.

The exhaust system comprised a chrome plated pipe, which ran down on the right, under the footrest, to the silencer. This was also plated and had its own unique shape, generated from two pressings welded together. In time, it became known as the 'flat Bantam' type and, as it did not dismantle, it tended to clog with oily deposits.

The petrol tank was formed from two main pressings, seam welded to a central section, the seams running along the tank top as a styling feature. The tank was held in place by two short bolts at the front, which ran into the sides of the headstock, and a single cross bolt at the rear. The quarter-turn filler cap incorporated a measure for the oil, which had to be mixed with the petrol, and the tank's capacity was $1\frac{3}{4}$ Imperial gallons.

The direct lighting system had a Wipac headlight fitted to an alloy shell, which also housed the switch

The Bantam engine could be used by other makes and for this one seems to have gained an alloy muff for the top of the barrel and another cylinder head.

D1 Bantams were a natural for the training scheme run by many British clubs in the post-war era and this one is at the Crystal Palace race track.

and a 3 volt dry battery for parking. The control for the switch was a lever mounted on the left handlebar and the two were connected by a cable. Switch positions were provided for off, parking, dipped and main headlight beam. At the rear was a small tubular lamp with a single-filament bulb.

The Bantam was finished in a Mist green colour that remained associated with it, becoming known as Bantam green. This was applied to virtually all parts, chrome plating being restricted to the exhaust system, handlebars, control levers and minor details. The petrol tank panels were finished in yellow with a transfer on each. At first, this was simply the well known BSA 'flying-wing', but it was soon amended to include the word 'Bantam' and a roundel picturing a cockerel.

By 1949 BSA were well into production with the model, which was listed as the D1, and it proved very popular everywhere it was sold. There were faults and weaknesses, but these tended to be nuisances rather than major problems, so could be lived with. For the rest, the Bantam offered a 50 mph top speed, 100 plus mpg economy without too much effort, fine handling and excellent brakes.

The stand was one item that could annoy the owner and lacked even the merit of being easy to use; a common problem for BSA. In time, it also failed to support either wheel off the ground or to hold the machine very securely at all. This arose because the stops on the stand and the frame stop plate dug into each other, as neither was really up to the job. In addition, the stand feet would wear away, which was aggravated by the machine then sliding back when parked to grind even more from the feet. Owners soon learned to cure the trouble by weld-ing extra material to the stand feet to start the whole process off again.

Both gear and rear brake pedals were set too high, and the latter used the same stop as the stand, so it could be affected by any wear or distortion of the stop. Jumping out of second has already been mentioned, along with the ratio gap to top, while a quirk concerned the flywheel discs. If the staking let go, these could spin freely in the crankcase and would do this with odd ringing noises if the engine stopped abruptly.

None of these points mattered too much in use, but the somewhat weak electrics did. The ignition was

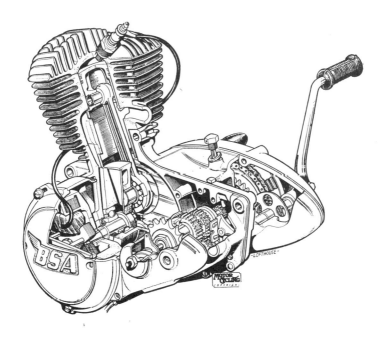

This is the 148 cc D3 Bantam Major engine which was very similar to the D1. It first appeared in 1954 when both had deeper fins for the head and barrel.

rather too dependent on the points gap and timing, while the internal coil was never really big enough for its job. The generating side was also marginal, so the lights gave limited illumination; quite normal then for a small two-stroke. Neither system liked the rain much, and both were prone to failure in the wet.

These points had no effect on the success of the Bantam, however, for it was very competitively priced at £60 plus purchase tax; just about rock bottom for a 125 cc machine at the time. Most others were powered by the much older Villiers engine, but an exception was the Royal Enfield which, like the BSA, was based on a pre-war DKW. However, in that case, it was the complete RT98 machine.

Variations - D1 & D3

Some of the minor problems were dealt with for 1950 with a string of alterations, beginning with a revised generator. At the same time, a range of D1 models was introduced with options for rear suspension and Lucas electrics, plus Competition versions as well.

The result was a total of eight possible combinations, thanks to the choice of Wipac or Lucas electrics for the engine in a rigid or plunger frame, this being repeated in Competition form. In practice, these last invariably had the Wipac ignition and usually the rigid frame, while the road model

with Lucas electrics would normally have the plunger frame.

All models had a new stand spring, so the retaining clip went, and an exhaust pipe which ran above the footrest bar. Gaiters appeared on the front forks, and the Wipac generator took on a new form with a much larger points cover, held by two screws. There was a simple wire lead exit in the upper rear quadrant of the stator for both low and high tension cables.

The Lucas option was rather more involved than appeared at first sight and introduced a battery, coil

Brochure picture of a 1957 D1 with its tubular silencer and battery lighting but still in the same Bantam mould.

A Bantam in later year, in this case a D3 with the heavier front forks and from the 1954-55 period so before pivoted fork rear suspension.

ignition and a rectifier. To control these, there was a combined lighting and ignition switch that went into a new headlamp shell, along with an ammeter and reduced-charge resistance. The rectifier was a massive selenium metal type, typical of its time and far removed from a modern component. The battery was hung next to the toolbox, which was moved over to make room for it, while the coil was fitted to a lug under the tank.

The final electrical change was to the generator, which was mounted to the much shortened end of the crankshaft. It comprised stator, rotor, outer race and points plate as a single assembly that was fitted to the crankcase side. This meant a change to that part to provide the mountings, plus a new magneto housing and points cover, a new mainshaft and heavier flywheels to balance the loss of rotor weight.

The plunger frame was much as others of its kind, with a fixed rod on each side for a slider carrying the wheel spindle. Load and rebound springs controlled its movement, but were undamped and concealed by steel covers, which often wore against each other. The wheel spindle size was increased to cope with the extra load, while the option also included a rear mudguard with a continuous valance and revised fixings.

The Competition models had a cylinder head with a second, forward, plug hole for a decompressor. Otherwise, they used the stock engine, but had a folding kickstart pedal and an exhaust pipe bent at the end to tilt the silencer up. On the chassis side, the saddle was raised on a frame and the footrests modified, while the front wheel was fitted with taper-roller bearings and the rear with a fatter-section tyre.

Finally, there were blade mudguards and a larger rear wheel sprocket to lower the gearing, which produced a bonus. This came from the resulting higher engine speed, which reduced the crankcase condensation that had been damaging the main bearings.

The Bantams were next altered for 1952, when the Wipac light switch was moved into the headlamp shell and the headstock gusset was strengthened. For 1953, the engine was fitted with wider big-end rollers, and the flywheels were recessed to accommodate them. The front mudguard lost its valance

Nearly the end of the line for the original style Bantam with this a 1962 D1 fitted with optional dual seat.

Ray Welman, winner of the Catalina Grand National 125 cc class in 1952 using an early D1 engine.

Hap Alzina, the major BSA importer stands on the right.

This is the 1957 version of the 148 cc D3 with pivoted fork rear suspension which was introduced the previous year.

and became unsprung, so was fitted to the lower fork legs, which had lugs added to suit. The tank seam welds were hidden under chrome-plated strips, and pillion footrest lugs were welded to the ` frame. A dual seat appeared as an option, although it was never to become standard for the rigid or plunger frame models, which remained faithful to the saddle to the end. The finish continued as Mist green, but with chrome-plated wheel rims, while an optional black

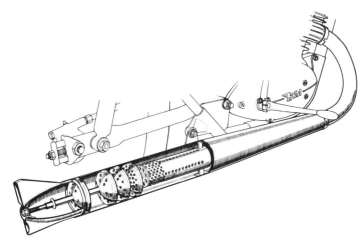

The new, long and tapered silencer which was introduced for the D3 in 1956 to replace the short tubular type.

scheme was also offered.

At the end of 1953, the Lucas options were dropped, but were replaced by equivalents with Wipac battery lighting, while the choice of rigid or plunger frames continued. With the direct lighting and Competition models in either frame, this made a total of six D1 Bantams, which were joined for 1954 by four D3 Bantam Major models fitted with a 148 cc engine. There were two of these for the road in the plunger frame with the choice of electrics,

models changed to a short tubular silencer with detachable fishtail, but the flat one remained on the Competition models. All lost the external gear indicator, which had always tended to fall off anyway. On the cycle side, the road models were given a headlamp cowl, and the D3 had heavier front forks and a larger front brake, which also went on the Competition D1.

The plunger frame Competition models were dropped for 1955, and at the end of that year the range

Brochure picture of the 1958 only 172 cc D5 which was based on the D3 cycle parts but fitted with a bigger engine.

and two more for competition with either frame type. The finish of all was in pastel grey with yellow tank panels. The larger capacity came from boring out the cylinder to 57 mm, and both head and barrel had a greater depth of finning compared to the early D1. The same fin increase appeared on the smaller engine, and both sizes of all road

was thinned right down. All the rigid and Competition models went, as did the D3 in the plunger frame, for that model moved on to a pivoted-fork frame (and, thus, the next chapter). This left the D1 in plunger frame with direct or battery Wipac lighting, and it was to continue in this form to the end of its days.

Only the finish varied, with a ma-

The D7 Bantam which replaced the D5 for 1959 and had new cycle parts but kept the 172 cc engine with one added side cover.

roon option joining the D1 green, D3 grey or optional black for 1955. These colours continued for the D1 to 1959. For 1960, the frame and most of the details became black, and only the petrol tank, mudguards and their stays were in colour with Mist green, Fuchsia red or black being the range of choice.

And so the D1 ran into 1963, when BSA dropped it from their range. They had a replacement, the four-stroke Beagle, but this was short-lived and never looked like having the charm or simplicity of the original. The Bantam continued in larger and heavier form, but it was the light and nippy D1 that was the real success story and the one most people remember.

It had served novices well and had been adopted as the mainstay of the Rider Training Scheme in Britain, so a great number of riders had taken their first nervous ride on one. The Post Office had used large numbers, painted in their traditional bright red and fitted with legshields, mainly used to prop the machine on a kerb, and a restricted throttle to reduce the speed at which they were dropped!

All this was lost and riders mourned the passing of an old friend.

Pivoted Fork - D3, D5 & D7

The Bantam story did not stop with the end of the D1, for the D3 continued and grew up into the D7. Back in 1956, it had switched to a pivoted-fork frame, and for that year was built into that alone, with direct or battery lighting.

The cycle parts were mainly new, but the engine unit was the D3 as before. The frame had a main single loop to which was bolted the subframe that supported the rear units and the dual seat, which was fitted as standard. The rear fork pivoted on Silentbloc rubber bushes pressed into its forward ends and on a fixed spindle, which picked up lugs on the subframe tubes, as well as the main one on the seat tube. The rear mudguard and chainguard

Main bearing lubrication using gearbox oil as adopted by the D7.

Bob Currie again, but this time out on a 1964 D7 Super de luxe Bantam and enjoying himself as much as always.

were new, as were the toolbox and side cover, which fitted into the corners of the subframe. The silencer became much longer and had a tapered front section leading into the tubular part.

The D3 was replaced by the 172 cc D5 for 1958, with the increase in capacity coming from a larger 61.5 mm bore. This meant a new cylinder, which had a flange mounting for the Amal Monobloc carburet-

tor, but otherwise was much as the others. The engine internals were altered to include a caged roller big end and the oil seals were re-arranged. The magneto seal stayed where it was, but another appeared inboard of the main bearing to isolate it from the crankcase. A similar seal appeared inboard of the drive side mains, but the one between them went, and all the mains were lubricated by the transmission

The 1965 D7 Super, still with the extra cover over the magneto.

The D7 Silver economy job introduced for 1966 with less chrome but the same engine as the de luxe model.

The 1966 Bantam D7 de luxe which had a better finish than the Silver and a higher price to suit.

oil, the crankcase being drilled with feed and drain holes.

The cycle parts were very much as for the 1956 D3 with few exceptions. One was the fuel tank, which was enlarged a little to 2 Imperial gallons, and another was the brakes.

Both of these had wider shoes than those of the D3, but the front one reverted to the 5 in. diameter of the D1. A further change was to 18 in. rims and 3.00 in.-section tyres in line with the trends of those times.

The D5 was available with direct

The economy D10 Silver which took over from the D7 in 1966 and had the points moved over to the right.

A four-speed gearbox went into the D10S Sportsman of 1966 which had further incentives to persuade the young rider to choose it.

or battery lighting and finished in Bayard crimson or black with ivory tank panels, but not for long. It was only listed for the one year before it was replaced by the D7 Super of the same capacity.

The revised machine used the same engine as before with the addition of a further cover for the left-hand side. This enclosed the magneto and clutch mechanism and

had the title 'Super' cast into it. The engine retained the same Amal Monobloc carburettor as the D5 and the long tapered silencer.

The cycle side was virtually all new, with a revised subframe being bolted to a modified main loop. The rear fork pivot was changed to a design where the pivot pin was pressed into the seat tube lug and bronze bushes were fitted in the

For trail use the Bantam was offered with the four-speed engine unit in this form as the D10B Bushman in the UK for 1966.

Bob again, this time on the three-speed D10 Supreme which offered a little more sparkle than the Silver.

fork forward ends. Outer plates helped to support the pin, but the result was no more effective than before and a great deal more difficult to service when worn.

At the front went new forks, based on Triumph Tiger Cub legs fitted to BSA yokes. The forks had hydraulic damping and a nacelle to carry the headlight and provide a mounting for the speedometer and light switch. Both wheels continued with the 3.00 x 18 in. tyres, but the cast-iron hubs came from the Cub and replaced the pressed steel of the earlier Bantam models. The rear sprocket was bolted, rather than riveted, in place and, thus, the Cub range of sprockets could be used if the owner wished. Both brakes were of the larger diameter and were also wider than in the past, while the mudguards were revised to suit the new frame and forks, as were the

The export trail D10 was listed as the Bushman Pastoral and differed from the home market one in a number of ways.

For 1968 the D14/4 replaced the D10 Supreme and used the four-speed engine unit and a larger diameter exhaust pipe.

handlebars. For the area under the dual seat nose, the toolbox and side cover were connected by a centre panel to produce a more enclosed space around the battery, coil and rectifier. The model was built with direct or battery lighting.

The finish of the D7 was in Royal red for the mudguards, toolbox, centre panel, side cover and the tank, which had ivory panels and a suitable 'Bantam Super' transfer, the rest of the painted parts being in black. There was also an all-black

The 1968 D14/4S Sportman was little altered from the D10 version and the D14 range was only built for one year.

Final D175 Bantam introduced in 1969 with this the following year's unchanged model.

option. For 1960, the colours became Signal red, blue or black, and for 1961, there was the option of chrome-plated tank side panels.

In 1962, the engine was fitted with a needle-roller small-end and the gearbox internal ratios were revised a little to raise first and reduce the gap between second and top. Two years later, the D7 was joined by a de luxe version; all had a revised si-lencer, twin switches for lights and ignition, and magnetic speedometer. Alongside the road models, there were also the D7 Trail and D7 Pastoral machines, which were built for export and off-road use. The Trail model used the early D1 forks and front wheel, with no headlamp, and both these models had an undershield and larger than usual air cleaner. The seat, tank and exhaust

Final Bantam engine unit, at last with a central plug, together with a good few other changes but at heart the same Bantam as always.

Last of the Bantam line and a good servant to its riders as it had been since 1948.

system also varied, depending on the model and the destination country.

For 1966, the two D7 road models were replaced by two more, which were listed as the D7 Silver and D7 de luxe. The former was an economy job with revised centre panels and tank shape that incor-porated knee recesses and round badges. These also went on the de luxe model, which had the better finish with chrome tank panels.

Both were replaced in July that year by the D10 range, which brought significant changes to the Bantam after some 50,000 of the D7 model had been built.

Four Speeds - D10, D14 & D175

The D10 Bantam range was announced in July 1966 with four models, two of which featured a very welcome four-speed gearbox. Otherwise, all were much as the D7, but a new six-pole Wipac alternator replaced the old unit and the points were moved to the right-hand end of the crankshaft.

The points cam was no longer keyed to the shaft, so ignition timing was less easy for the rider to set, and the primary chaincase was amended to carry the points plate. A small cover enclosed the details and was held by two screws. The engine itself had a larger carburettor fitted which, along with an increase in compression ratio, raised the power output, demanding an extra plate in the clutch.

Some early D10 machines had Monobloc carburettors, but most came with the Concentric type that replaced it, and all but one had a pancake air filter fitted.

The three-speed models were the Silver and Supreme, which effectively replaced the two D7 machines. The four-speed ones were the Sports and Bushman, both of which came in two forms with minor changes and were called the Sportsman and Bushman Pastoral respectively for the USA and export markets.

For the four-speed models, the crankcase was revised to accept the new gear cluster, which was in the British form with one gear on each shaft moved from side-to-side to select the ratios. These

The D175B Bushman built using the same engine unit and mainly similar cycle parts as the road model.

The great Brian Stonebridge riding the Bantam he helped to develop so well.

The Bantam trials machine built in 1967 by the factory with a view to production which was not to come.

were controlled by forks on a rod. A camplate moved these and was itself geared to the positive-stop mechanism, which was all new, but terminated in the same gear pedal as before. The kickstart mechanism was unchanged, but the sleeve gear oil seal now had its housing cast as part of the left-hand crankcase and there was a needle-roller thrust race for the clutch, while the flanged bush became a bush and separate thrust washer. The three-speed models

did not receive any of these changes.

Finish of the D10 Silver was in Sapphire blue for the mudguards and centre panels, the tank also being blue, but with gold lined, silver panels carrying round tank badges. The Supreme was similar, but in flamboyant blue with parts of the tank side panels chrome-plated and white lining for the tank and mudguards. The model was fitted with twin mirrors and ball-ended control levers to enhance its specification from that of the Silver.

The D10 Sports model had a waist-level exhaust system with a small heat shield on the silencer, separate headlamp shell carrying the speedometer and switches, fly screen, dual seat with hump and full width hubs. The finish was as for the Supreme, but in red, and the mudguards and headlamp shell were chrome plated. The Sportsman for the USA differed in its handlebars and mudguards, which were not drilled, as no number plates were fitted, and it was supplied without the fly screen.

The D10 Bushman was an off-road, or trail, machine, so it had suitable tyres on 19 in. rims. The exhaust was again upswept, but had a longer heat shield, while a flat dual seat was fitted, although a short single one appeared on the export Pastoral version, which was not supplied with pillion rests. Both had an undershield, gaitered forks and offset hubs, while the Pastoral had a rear carrier. The rear hub continued with the bolted on sprocket, but the gearing varied; 47 teeth for the Bushman and 58 for the Pastoral.

The Pastoral also had a different air cleaner with an element in a housing connected by hose to the carburettor. This assembly was fitted under the right-hand side cover, so all the centre panels differed. Both used the same fuel tank, which was painted in Bushfire orange and white, with just a transfer on each side. The orange was also used for the centre panels. The Bushman headlamp was the same as that on the Sports model, but the Pastoral one was smaller with direct lighting and a black finish.

Late in 1967, the D10 models became the D14 series and three in number. The early machines had a D13 prefix for both engine and frame numbers, but this was

Early Bantam racing with John Hogan flat out on his rigid frame machine and winning as he usually did.

A 1958 picture and the racer has a Hogan head and Pigrim oil pump, then a popular fitting while the megaphone exhaust was usual.

never a model and the D14 prefix was soon adopted. All had the four-speed gearbox plus a larger-diameter exhaust pipe and raised compression ratio. The models were the D14/4 Supreme, D14/4S Sports and D14/4B Bushman, the last two being fitted with heavier-duty front forks and a front brake backplate with torque arm. The road models changed to an air cleaner fitted under the right-hand side panel and connected to the carburettor by hose, while the Bushman continued with the system used by the D10 Pastoral.

The Supreme kept the fork nacelle and offset hubs, while the Sports stayed with the full-width type and its other features of raised exhaust system, humped dual seat and fly screen. The Bushman was altered with a full-width front hub only, but kept to its larger rim size and was only offered with the dual seat. The finishes of all three were as for the D10 models with the addition of an all-black option for the Supreme.

If anything, the D14 series had a shorter life than the D10, for it was replaced by just two models for 1969. These were the D175 road and Bushman machines, which were to be the last of the line. They were also referred to as the Bantam 175, hence B175, and Bushman 175 at various times but D175 and D175B seem to be the more official designations.

For the two models, the engine was amended with new crankcase castings and a cylinder head with a central sparking plug. Inside went a modified crankshaft, but otherwise the details were as before. Externally, the road model had a low-level exhaust pipe and silencer, while the Bushman had the same items at waist level, plus a long heat shield, and kept its folding kickstart pedal.

The cycle side of the two machines was as for the earlier ones, both using the same flat dual seat and similar tank, although the road model retained the round plastic tank badges. Both machines had a separate headlamp shell with the speedometer installed in it, but with two switches for the road model and only one for the Bushman. Both went back to offset hubs, but kept the gaitered forks. The road machines had rear unit covers, but no undershield, and the Bushman was the reverse.

The mudguards were in touring style and painted for the road, but were white and sporting for trail use. Accessories such as legshields, crashbars, rear carrier and panniers continued to be offered, much as always. The finish was in blue, red or black for the road model, while retaining the chrome-plated tank panels, and the Bushman remained in orange and white.

This was the final form of the Bantam, which entered the 1970s without any real change. Sadly, its days were numbered, and only the road model was included in the last major launch for 1971. By March that year, it had faded from the lists and, in time, its jigs were destroyed, while the firm itself failed.

Thus came the end for one of the best loved and most successful of all British motorcycles, which had helped countless thousands make their first tentative forays on to the roads. Few post-war riders had not owned or ridden one at some time or another, and with the classic revival of the 1980s, it is as popular as ever. Then it was your first road machine, now it is the first restoration tackled by many, for, as always, it is an easy job to handle.

The author's Bantam in 1962 with points moved inboard and expansion exhaust.

Bantams in Competition

Almost as soon as the Bantam was launched, some owners were altering them for competition use on or off the road. The factory was equally quick off the mark with machines running in trials and scrambles events in 1949, while a year later, the Competition model was listed for the public.

It remained until 1955 and was joined by the D3 version for the last couple of years. Even when withdrawn, the factory continued with them for a year or two, but then abandoned them in favour of their more usual four-strokes. In the 1960s, they used an adapted D10, and there were other trials projects, both from BSA and firms such as Comerfords. None, however, produced more than a few machines.

The situation was rather different with road racing, where the factory had no real involvement, but many hundreds of machines were built up over the years. It began in 1949 with a single entry at Silverstone, and in the following year, 125 cc races began to be held regularly in Britain with John Hogan doing most of the winning with his Bantam. To their eternal credit, BSA did produce sets of close-ratio gears for the Bantam, and this encouraged quite a number of riders to tune the small two-stroke. The factory also made wide-ratio sets and other combinations, one of which makes a very nice road set with a mildly-tuned engine.

Hogan continued to dominate his class in 1951, but moved on to other makes soon after. During the rest of the 1950s period, the BSA model was raced in a supporting role in Britain, but on the other side of the world the Austra-

Bantam racing in the 1970's had moved onto machines such as this successful one.

Fred Launchbury dominated Bantam racing for many years and is here seen at Silverstone in 1966.

lians were running their machines on alcohol fuel and getting some very good results indeed. Back home in 1960, the scene changed when the Bantam Racing Club was formed, holding its first meeting in the following year.

This proved extremely success-ful, and within a few years, the club was promoting up to ten events annually, and large numbers of Bantams were being well tuned for them. Some even went on to run in the TT, but most stayed with the club, where some hard and fast racing took place, providing a good grounding for novice riders.

This racing showed just how good the basic design was, as the fastest of the early machines used stock parts, the speed coming from changes of piston, head and car-burettor, plus conventional tun-ing. Practically all machines used the three-speed gearbox, which gave the clutch a hard time, but there was one close-ratio, four-speed box from the factory, while one member combined two boxes to arrive at a six-speed selection.

Bantam racing declined to a de-gree when the factory closed, but continued in the 1980s. By then, the classic revival was well un-derway, so the source of machines began to dry up and the Bantam no longer offered cheap racing. In the past, the club had even bought them back from the Post Office for members, but those days went and the machines became more valuable for restoration. Old racers hunted their sheds for the parts that had been discarded in the search for speed and were now in short supply and valuable. Few had thought that flat silencers, toolboxes and shovel front mud-guards would ever have been so sought after.

So the Bantam continued to give pleasure to owners as it had done for so many years.

Bantam Specifications

Model	D1	D1	D1	D1comp	D3	D3
years	1948-55	1950-63	1950-53	1950-55	1954-55	1956-57
electrics	Wipac	Wipac	Lucas	Wipac	Wipac	Wipac
frame	rigid	plunger	plunger	rigid	plunger	s/a
no.cylinders	1	1	1	1	1	1
bore mm	52	52	52	52	57	57
stroke mm	58	58	58	58	58	58
capacity cc	123	123	123	123	148	148
comp. ratio	6.5	6.5	6.5	6.5	6.4	6.4
carb size	5/8	5/8	5/8	5/8	11/16	11/16
no.gears	3	3	3	3	3	3
top gear	7.0	7.0	7.0	8.64	7.0	7.0
petrol - gall	1.75	1.75	1.75	1.75	1.75	1.75
front tyre	2.75x19	2.75x19	2.75x19	2.75x19	2.75x19	2.75x19
rear tyre	2.75x19	2.75x19	2.75x19	3.25x19	2.75x19	2.75x19
front brake dia	5	5	5	5[1]	5	5
rear brake dia	5	5	5	5	5	5
wheelbase in.	50	50	50	50	50	51

[1] 1954-55 $5\frac{1}{2}$

Bantam Specifications

Model	D3comp	D5	D7	D10	D10S	D10B
years	1954-55	1958	1959-66	1966-67	1966-67	1966-67
frame	rigid	s/a	s/a	s/a	s/a	s/a
no.cylinders	1	1	1	1	1	1
bore mm	57	61.5	61.5	61.5	61.5	61.5
stroke mm	58	58	58	58	58	58
capacity cc	148	172	172	172	172	172
comp. ratio	6.4	7.4	7.4	8.65	8.65	8.65
carb size	11/16	7/8	7/8	26 mm	26 mm	26 mm
no.gears	3	3	3	3	4	4
top gear	8.64	6.43	6.43[2]	6.57	6.57	8.1
petrol - gall	1.75	2.0	2.0[3]	1.87	1.87	1.87
front tyre	2.75x19	3.00x18	3.00x18	3.00x18	3.00x18	3.00x19
rear tyre	3.25x19	3.00x18	3.00x18	3.00x18	3.00x18	3.00x19
front brake dia	$5\frac{1}{2}$	5	$5\frac{1}{2}$	$5\frac{1}{2}$	$5\frac{1}{2}$	$5\frac{1}{2}$
rear brake dia	5	5	$5\frac{1}{2}$	$5\frac{1}{2}$	$5\frac{1}{2}$	$5\frac{1}{2}$
wheelbase in.	50	52	51.1	50	50	50

[2] 1962-66 - 6.57, [3] 1966 - 1.87

Bantam Specifications

Model	D14/4	D14/4S	D14/4B	D175	D175B
years	1968	1968	1968	1969-71	1969-70
frame	s/a	s/a	s/a	s/a	s/a
no.cylinders	1	1	1	1	1
bore mm	61.5	61.5	61.5	61.5	61.5
stroke mm	58	58	58	58	58
capacity cc	172	172	172	172	172
comp. ratio	10.0	10.0	10.0	9.5	9.5
carb size	26 mm	26 mm	26 mm	26 mm	26 mm
no. gears	4	4	4	4	4
top gear	6.57	6.57	8.1	6.57	8.1
petrol - gall	1.87	1.87	1.87	1.87	1.87
front tyre	3.00x18	3.00x18	3.00x19	3.00x18	3.00x19
rear tyre	3.00x18	3.00x18	3.00x19	3.00x18	3.25x18
front brake dia	$5\frac{1}{2}$	$5\frac{1}{2}$	$5\frac{1}{2}$	$5\frac{1}{2}$	$5\frac{1}{2}$
rear brake dia	$5\frac{1}{2}$	$5\frac{1}{2}$	$5\frac{1}{2}$	$5\frac{1}{2}$	$5\frac{1}{2}$
wheelbase in.	50	50	50	50	50